Digital Photography Guide

A Step-by-Step Blueprint to Master Camera Settings, Composition, and Natural Lighting—Capture Pro-Quality Shots with Any DSLR or Mirrorless Camera

Marc T. Billy

Contents

Introduction V

1. Photography Without Intimidation 1
2. Unlocking the Camera Brain — Exposure Made Easy 6
3. Focus & Sharpness — How the Pros Get It Right 14
4. Composition — How to Make Every Photo Visually Powerful 21
5. Light Is Everything — Mastering Natural & Artificial Lighting 27
6. Portraits & People — Creating Emotion and Connection 34
7. Landscapes & Travel — Telling Stories Through Scenes 41
8. Everyday Photography — Finding Beauty in the Ordinary 48
9. Intro to Photo Editing — Enhance Without Overdoing It 54
10. Building Your Photography Confidence & Style 61
11. BONUS CHAPTER 67

Acknowledgements 73

About the author 75

Introduction

The Difference Between a Camera Owner and a Photographer

You picked up a camera because something inside you whispered, *"You can do this."*

Maybe it was a moment. A sunrise. A face. A feeling.
Something so powerful or beautiful that you felt the urge to capture it—forever.

But then you hit a wall.
Maybe it was the buttons. The menus. The endless YouTube rabbit holes.
Maybe your photos came out blurry, too dark, or too dull—nothing like the vibrant, magazine-worthy images that inspired you to begin in the first place.

And slowly, the voice that once whispered, *"You can do this,"* began to fade beneath louder doubts:
"Maybe I'm not cut out for this."
"Maybe I'm just not technical enough."
"Maybe I need a better camera."

Stop right there.
Because the truth is simpler and far more powerful than you've been led to believe:

> You don't need more gear. You need more guidance.

Not complicated charts. Not confusing manuals.
You need someone to show you—not tell you—how to unlock the camera in your hand, the vision in your head, and the story in your heart.

That's what this book is.

Why This Book Exists

There are thousands of photography books out there.

Some of them are brilliant. Many are bloated.
And most assume you're already fluent in f-stops, histograms, and tech talk.

But what if you're not?

What if you just want someone to walk you through things in plain language?
What if you want to *understand* how to take great photos—not by memorizing settings, but by truly seeing the world like a photographer?

That's where *Digital Photography Mastery* comes in.

This isn't a book full of fluff or theory.
It's a **hands-on field guide**—a companion you can carry (literally or mentally) every time you pick up your camera.

Each chapter in this book is a step forward.

- Not overwhelming.
- Not rushed.
- Just one concept at a time, taught like a trusted friend would teach it.

By the time you finish, you won't just know what to do—you'll know why it works, how to trust your instincts, and when to break the rules like an artist.

What You'll Learn—And Why It Matters

We start at the very beginning. As if you know nothing.
Because that's exactly how you should start—with zero shame, zero pressure, and all the wonder in the world.

Here's a glimpse of what you'll discover inside:

- How to finally make sense of aperture, shutter speed, and ISO (in under 20 minutes)
- How to blur backgrounds, freeze motion, and make every photo look *intentional*
- How to use light—any light—to your advantage, whether you're indoors, outdoors, or under the worst conditions
- How to shoot stunning portraits, breathtaking landscapes, and everyday magic
- How to train your eye to see like a photographer—even

before you raise your camera

- And how to edit your photos in a way that *enhances* them, not masks them

And no—none of this requires an expensive camera.
You can do everything in this book with a basic DSLR or mirrorless setup and a willingness to play, practice, and notice what others miss.

A Journey That Respects You

If you've ever felt talked down to…
If you've ever quit because things got too complicated…
If you've ever looked at someone else's photo and thought, *"Why don't mine look like that?"*

This book was written for you.

You are not behind. You are not too old. You are not "non-technical."
You are a human being with a camera. And that's all we need to begin.

> **This is your moment.** To slow down. To look closer. To learn not just how to use your camera—but how to see again.

Not with your eyes, but with intention. With wonder. With clarity.

You've been a camera owner.
Now, it's time to become a photographer.

Chapter 1

Photography Without Intimidation

The Gentle Beginning That Makes All the Difference

You hold something in your hands that's far more powerful than it looks.
A device that can freeze time.
A tool that turns fleeting moments into something permanent, meaningful—even unforgettable.

And yet… you may have found yourself staring down at your camera or phone, overwhelmed. Frustrated. Confused. Maybe even ready to give up.

All those buttons. All those modes. All those voices online telling you to shoot in manual, to "get it right in camera," to buy more gear, to stop being a beginner.

But there's something no one ever tells you at the start: You're not supposed to know what you're doing yet. You're not late. You're right on time.

The fact that you've opened this book—whether you're holding it in your lap or scrolling through it on a screen—means you're ready for more than just casual snapshots. You're here because you want to understand what makes a *great* photo great… and how to make one yourself.

Let me say this clearly:
You **can** learn this.
You do **not** need to be a tech expert.
And it is **not** too late to become a photographer—one who shoots with intention, clarity, and creative confidence.

The Trap of "Better Gear"

Let's address the myth first: *better photos don't come from better cameras.*
They come from better understanding.

Some of the most powerful photographs in history were taken with cameras that are, by today's standards, laughably simple. What they had wasn't 8K resolution or facial recognition autofocus. They had **vision.** They had **timing.** And they had the ability to see what others missed.

That's what this book is going to teach you—not how to memorize settings, but how to see like a photographer.

What This Chapter Will Give You

This chapter is not about buttons, specs, or comparing camera brands. That will come later.
Right now, we need to do something much more important:

- **Disarm the fear.**
- **Unravel the confusion.**

- **And rebuild your confidence from the ground up.**

This is about starting with the right *mindset*. Because no technique, no lens, no YouTube tutorial will matter if you're constantly second-guessing your ability to improve.

Let's start by shifting the way you see yourself.

You're Not a "Beginner." You're Becoming.

Photography isn't a competition. It's not a race. It's not a status. It's a practice. A personal one.

And yet, so many people quit before they ever find their rhythm—why?

Because they're made to feel small for not knowing the difference between aperture and ISO.
Because they shot on "Auto" and were told that wasn't good enough.
Because they felt embarrassed asking simple questions in advanced forums.

> No one should feel ashamed of where they are in their learning journey. This chapter—this whole book—exists to be your **safe place to begin.**

You Don't Need Fancy Gear (Here's What You *Do* Need)

Let's talk honestly. You do **not** need a $3,000 camera to make beautiful images.

You only need:

- A camera (DSLR, mirrorless, or even a good smartphone)
- Something to photograph (literally anything around you)
- A desire to understand how your camera "thinks"
- The patience to slow down and observe

If you have those, you're ready.
Everything else—lenses, lights, and editing tools—are just accessories to support your growth, not define it.

> Don't let the internet convince you that yourar isn't "pro" enough.
> Some of the most soulful, captivating shots come from fromlimited tools—and unlimited curiosity.

What Makes a Photographer Different from Everyone Else?

It's not their gear. It's not their training.
It's how they **see.**

A photographer walks into a room and notices the light on someone's cheek.
They pass a brick wall and pause—not because the bricks are interesting, but because the shadows tell a story.
They understand that even the most ordinary moment—a coffee cup, a sidewalk, a face in motion—can be transformed through perspective.

And here's the beautiful truth:
You're already wired to notice these things. You've just forgotten how.

This book will remind you.

Let's Unlock What's Already Inside You

So here's my invitation to you—not as a teacher, but as a fellow traveler on this journey:

Let go of the need to be perfect.
Forget about getting every photo "right."
Release the fear of manual mode, and let's focus on learning the language of light, timing, and composition—together.

Every chapter in this book will take you deeper into your understanding of what makes a photo not just technically correct, but emotionally *alive.*

And we'll do it simply. Clearly. Practically.
One concept at a time. One skill at a time.

Because the best way to learn photography…
It is not by rushing.
It's by *seeing.*

And today, your eyes are open.

Let's keep going.

Chapter 2

Unlocking the Camera Brain — Exposure Made Easy

Let's begin with a fundamental truth: the camera doesn't care what you're photographing.
It doesn't know if you're shooting a golden sunset or your daughter's first dance recital. It doesn't understand emotion, timing, or the beauty of a moment. It's just a machine—one that's programmed to measure **light** and respond accordingly.

But *you*? You see the scene. You feel it.
You're not just taking pictures. You're interpreting light, freezing life, and telling a story.

And that's why understanding **exposure** is the single most important leap you'll make as a photographer.

What Is Exposure—Really?

Think of exposure as the balance between *light* and *dark* in your photo.
Too much light, and everything looks washed out and lifeless.
Too little, and your subject disappears into the shadows.

Perfect exposure? It's when the image feels just right—clear, detailed, and full of the mood you intended to capture.

But exposure isn't one fixed setting.
It's the result of three decisions your camera makes—or that you take control of. Together, these three elements form what photographers call the **Exposure Triangle:**

- Aperture—How wide the lens opens to let in light
- **Shutter Speed—**How long the sensor is exposed to light
- ISO—How sensitive the sensor is to light

Let's unpack them in the simplest, most visual way possible.

Imagine the Camera as a Window

To understand exposure, imagine a room with a single window and a curtain.

- **Aperture** is how wide the window opens.
- **Shutter speed** is how long you leave the curtain open.
- **ISO** is how sensitive your eyes are to the light coming in.

You can let in more light by opening the curtain wider (aperture), leaving it open longer (shutter speed), or adjusting your eyes to see better in the dark (ISO).

Now, translate that to your camera.

Aperture: The Gateway to Light & Blur

Aperture refers to the **size of the opening inside your lens.** This opening controls not just brightness but also **depth of field**—how much of the image is in focus.

It's measured in **f-stops:** f/1.8, f/2.8, f/5.6, f/11, f/22, and so on.

Here's the tricky part: **the smaller the f-number, the wider the opening.**
Think of it like golf—lower numbers mean bigger impact.

What a Wide Aperture Does (f/1.8–f/4):

- Lets in *more* light (great for low-light situations)
- Creates a **shallow depth of field** (blurry backgrounds—perfect for portraits)

What a Narrow Aperture Does (f/8–f/22):

- Lets in *less* light (needs brighter conditions or longer exposure)
- Creates a **deeper depth of field** (everything in focus—ideal for landscapes)

Real Example: Take a photo of your friend at f/2.8, and the background melts into a soft blur.
Take that same shot at f/11, and suddenly the trees, buildings, or other ordistractions behind them are crystal clear.

The aperture gives you **creative control** over where the eye goes.

Shutter Speed: The Motion Freezer (or Motion Blurrer)

Shutter speed controls **how long the sensor is exposed to light.** A faster shutter means the photo is taken quickly, freezing motion. A slower shutter allows more light in but risks blur.

Shutter speeds are measured in fractions of a second:

- **Fast:** 1/1000, 1/500, 1/250
- **Medium:** 1/125, 1
- **Slow:** 1/30, 1 second, 5 seconds+

Use Fast Shutter Speeds When:

- Capturing sports, pets, kids—anything moving fast
- Shooting handheld in daylight
- You want crystal-clear, frozen moments

Use Slow Shutter Speeds When:

- Photographing at night or indoors without a flash

- Capturing motion blur (waterfalls, light trails, star trails)
- Using a tripod for long-exposure creativity

> Pro Insight: If your photo looks a little soft and you're handholding your camera, your shutter speed might be too slow.
> The general rule? Always shoot at 1 over **your focal length.** (Using a 50mm lens?)? Try not to go below 1/50 handheld.)

ISO: The Brightness Booster (With a Catch)

ISO controls your camera's **sensitivity to light.**
The higher the ISO, the brighter the image—*but* at a cost.

ISO is typically measured in 100, 200, 400, 800, 1600, 3200, etc.

When to Use Low ISO (100–400):

- Outdoors during the day
- In well-lit environments
- When image quality matters most

When to Use Higher ISO (800+):

- Indoors, nighttime, or low light
- When you need a faster shutter speed
- If it's better to have some grain than miss the shot.

Important: Higher ISO = more noise (grainy look). But with modern cameras, shooting up to 1600–3200 is often totally usable—especially for social sharing or black-and-white editing.

The Balance: How to Actually Use the Triangle

Here's where it gets exciting. Every shot is a **balancing act.**

Let's say you want to take a beautiful portrait:

- You want a **blurry background** → choose a wide aperture (f/2.8)
- But now there's too much light → increase shutter speed (1/500)
- Or you're indoors and the shot's too dark → bump ISO from 200 to 800

It's a dance between light, movement, and detail.

You don't always have to shoot in full manual. You can start with:

- **Aperture Priority (A or Av)—You** control blur; the camera handles the rest
- **Shutter Priority (S or Tv)—You** control motion; the camera balances brightness
- **Manual Mode (M)—You're** the boss of everything

Real-World Practice (You Can Try This Today)

Try this at home:

1. Set your camera to Aperture Priority mode (A or Av)
2. Set ISO to 200
3. Take three photos of the same object:
    - First at **f/2.8**
    - Then at **f/5.6**
    - Then at **f/11**
4. Look at the background in each image. See how it changes? That's **depth of field** in action.

Do the same using Shutter Priority. Try:

- 1/1000 (freeze)
- 1/60 (balanced)
- 1/10 (motion blur—try with moving water or your hand)

This is how you train your instincts. Not with theory, but with observation.

Final Thought: You're Not Controlling a Machine. You're Sculpting Light.

What makes this exciting isn't just the technical mastery—it's the **creative control.**

- Want emotion? Blur the background.
- Want impact? Freeze the action.
- Want mood? Embrace the shadows.

Now that you understand how your camera *thinks*, you can begin to **tell it what to do**—instead of hoping it gets it right.

And the next time someone says, "Wow, that photo amazing... How did you do it?"
You'll smile, because now... you'll know.

Chapter 3

Focus & Sharpness — How the Pros Get It Right

There's nothing more disappointing than reviewing a beautiful image—perfect lighting, perfect timing—and realizing it's slightly… off.

Just soft enough to ruin it.
The focus missed. The details are lost. The moment, gone.

If you've been there, take heart. You're not failing—you're learning.
Sharpness is not a luxury in photography—it's the foundation of trust in your images. And contrary to what most people think, getting consistently sharp photos isn't about luck or gear. It's about knowing how focus works and how to work with it—not against it.

This chapter is your blueprint.

What *Is* Focus, Exactly?

Focus determines which part of your photo is sharp and clear. Everything outside that focused area begins to blur—and that's not always a bad thing.

- In **portraits**, we *want* the background blurred so the eyes stand out.
- In **landscapes**, we often want the entire frame sharp—from the grass to the mountaintop.

But before you can control focus creatively, you have to master it *functionally*.

Autofocus vs. Manual Focus

Your camera has two ways of focusing:

Autofocus (AF)

This is what most people use, and for good reason—it's fast, smart, and usually very accurate.

Modern cameras let you choose between autofocus **modes** (how the camera behaves) and **points** (where the camera focuses).

Manual Focus (MF)

This is where *you* turn the focus ring on your lens to find sharpness yourself. It's great for still objects, close-ups, or low-light scenes where autofocus can struggle.

Start here: Stick with autofocus for now. You'll learn manual focus later when you need more precision.

The 3 Autofocus Modes (And When to Use Them)

1. **Single Shot AF (AF-S or One Shot AF)**
   - Best for still subjects: portraits, food, landscapes
   - You press the shutter halfway to lock focus, then shoot
2. **Continuous AF (AF-C or AI Servo)**
   - Best for moving subjects: pets, kids, sports
   - Camera continually adjusts focus as the subject moves
3. **Auto AF (AF-A or AI Focus)**
   - Camera chooses between single and continuous
   - Often works fine, but not as predictable as choosing yourself

> **Pro insight: For portraits and posed photos, use Single Shot AF. For anything that moves—even slightly—switch to Continuous AF to track your subject.**

Focus Points — The Secret to Precision

Your camera has **focus points**—little dots or squares that light up when you focus.

You can:

- **Let the camera choose** a focus point (not recommended—it often chooses wrong)

- **Manually select one** (highly recommended for control)

Here's the golden rule:

Always put the focus point on what you want sharpest. For portraits, that's *the eye.* For landscapes, that's *roughly one-third into the scene.* For close-ups, it's *the exact detail you want to highlight.*

Don't trust your camera to guess what matters. You tell it.

Standing Still Isn't Always Enough

Camera shake is one of the most common reasons sharp photos turn out… not sharp.

Even if your subject is still, *you* might be moving slightly—especially in low light or when using slow shutter speeds.

Simple Stability Tips:

- Use two hands, elbows tucked in
- Brace against a wall or lean into your body
- Breathe out gently before pressing the shutter
- Use a tripod when shooting below 1/60s
- Use your camera's **image stabilization (IS/VR/IBIS)** when available

Memory Tip: "1 over focal length" Shooting with a 50mm lens? Keep shutter speed at 1/50 sec or faster. Using 100mm? Go 1/100 sec or faster.

Focus Lock — A Beginner's Power Move

Let's say you want your subject **off-center** (which looks more dynamic than center framing), but the only focus point is in the middle.

Here's what to do:

1. Point the center focus square **at the subject's eye**
2. Press the shutter halfway to lock focus
3. While holding it halfway, **recompose** your shot
4. Then press the shutter fully to take the photo

This is called **focus and recompose**—a trick pros use constantly.

Depth of Field: Why Some Photos Are Sharp Front to Back

Depth of field (DoF) is the distance between the **nearest and farthest** objects in a scene that appear in focus.

Controlled by your **aperture**, it determines whether:

- Only the subject is sharp and the background melts (shallow DoF)

- Or everything, near to far, looks sharp (deep DoF)

We covered aperture in the last chapter, but here's how it applies here:

Aperture Depth of Field Best f/1.8–f/2.8 Very shallow Portraits, soft background f/4–f/5.6 Medium Close-ups, travel, events –f/16 Deep Landscapes, architecture

Rule of thumb: Want *only* the subject sharp? Go wide (f/2.8). Want everything sharp? Go narrow (f/11+).

Quick Practice: From Blurry to Brilliant

Try this exercise:

1. Place a coffee mug on a table with some distance behind it
2. Set your camera to Aperture Priority (A/Av)
3. Choose f/2.8 and focus on the mug → take the shot
4. Now choose f/8 and shoot again
5. Then try f/16 → shoot once more

Review the photos.

- What changes in the background?
- How sharp is the subject?
- Where is your focus point in each image?

This kind of hands-on play builds confidence *fast.*

Final Word: Sharpness Isn't Perfection. It's Clarity.

What separates a "decent" photo from one that *stops someone scrolling* is often just this: **intentional focus.**

You don't have to be perfect. You don't need razor-sharp results every time.

But when you begin to choose *what* is sharp—and why—your photos stop feeling accidental. They begin to feel **crafted.**

That's the shift. That's the power.

And now that you can focus with confidence, we're ready to unlock the secret behind every great image: **composition.**

Chapter 4

Composition — How to Make Every Photo Visually Powerful

When someone looks at a photograph and says, *"Wow, that's beautiful,"* they're often reacting to something they can't quite explain. It's not the camera. It's not the technical settings. It's something deeper—*how* the image was framed.

That's the quiet art of **composition.**
It's the difference between a photo that tells a story… and one that just fills the frame.

And here's the secret: composition has nothing to do with how expensive your camera is.
It's about where you stand, what you include, what you leave out, and what you choose to *say* with your shot.

This chapter will teach you how to see the frame like an artist.
Not with rules, but with intention.

What Is Composition?

Composition is simply **how you arrange elements within the frame.**

It's not about rules—it's about decisions.

- What's the subject?
- Where is it placed?
- What's happening in the background?
- Is the viewer's eye being guided… or lost?

Every time you press the shutter, you're making a choice:
This is what matters. This is what I want you to see.

Start Here: Slow Down and Ask

Before you even raise your camera, ask:

- What am I drawn to?
- Why does this moment matter?
- What do I want to include—or remove?

Photography isn't about pressing the button fast.
It's about noticing what others overlook. And choosing *how* to show it.

The Rule of Thirds (And Why It Works)

If you learn nothing else about composition, start with this.

Imagine your image is divided into a grid with **two vertical** and **two horizontal** lines, like a tic-tac-toe board.

Now, place your **subject at one of the four intersections.**

This simple shift away from center:

- Creates balance
- Draws the eye naturally
- Adds elegance and tension to your frame

***Why it works:* The human eye loves structure. But perfect symmetry gets boring fast. By offsetting the subject, you create energy—without chaos.**

Composition Techniques That Work Every Time

Let's walk through techniques used by professionals—not as rigid "rules," but as flexible tools in your creative kit.

1. Leading Lines

Use roads, railings, fences, shadows, or architecture to draw the viewer's eye toward your subject.

2. Framing Within a Frame

Shoot through doorways, windows, trees, or arches to create a "picture-in-picture" effect. It adds depth and focus.

3. Negative Space

Leave empty space around your subject.
It makes the image breathe. It creates mood, simplicity, and strength.

4. Symmetry & Reflections

Use symmetry when you want power, calm, or beauty—especially in nature or architecture. Reflections in water, mirrors, or glass are powerful composition tools.

5. Texture & Patterns

Zoom in close and let repeating patterns or textures (bricks, leaves, fabric, skin) tell their own quiet story.

6. Fill the Frame

Get in close. Don't be afraid to crop. Remove distractions. Let the subject dominate the shot.

Break the Rules When It Feels Right

You don't *have* to follow any of these ideas. Sometimes the best photos happen when you break them—*on purpose.*

Blur the subject. Off-center the focus. Cut off a part of the frame. It's all valid… if it's done with intention.

> Composition isn't about doing it "right." It's about making the viewer feel something.

Vertical vs. Horizontal (Portrait vs. Landscape)

This simple choice changes the entire feel of your photo.

- **Horizontal (landscape):** Calm, expansive, wide view—best for scenes, group shots, environment
- **Vertical (portrait):** Intimate, tight, focused—best for people, details, lines, drama

Try both. Always. Don't default. Decide.

Real- Framing the Mundane"

Exercise:
Choose an object you see every day: a coffee mug, your shoes, or a doorway.

Now, take 10 different photos of it using the composition techniques above:

- Frame it through something
- Use shadows or light as leading lines
- Try it on the left, then the right, then dead center
- Shoot it close, then with space
- Try symmetry, then tilt the angle

This exercise will teach you how to turn the *ordinary* into *art*—simply by where you place your subject.

The Photographer's Eye Is Always Cropping

Train yourself to look at the world like a photo—always asking:

- What's in the background?

- Is there clutter I can step away from?
- Can I shoot from lower, higher, or from behind?

You don't need Photoshop to "fix" your composition.
You just need a few extra seconds before clicking.

That's the difference between a snapshot and a story.

Final Thought: The Frame Is Your Voice

Imagine someone handing you a blank canvas and saying,
"Tell me what matters."

That's what every photograph is.

It's not just about focus, or light, or gear.
It's about **where you choose to place your attention.**
Because where you put the subject… is where the viewer puts their heart.

> You don't need perfect technique.
> You need presence.
> Composition is how you take control of the conversation between your photo and the person looking at it.

And now that you can compose with clarity, it's time to tackle the most powerful creative force in photography:

Light.

Chapter 5

Light Is Everything — Mastering Natural & Artificial Lighting

You can have the best gear in the world. You can know every setting, every trick.
But if you don't understand light—if you can't *see* it, shape it, or feel it—your photos will always fall flat.

Photography, at its core, is just this: **writing with light.**
And the more fluently you speak that language, the more visually powerful your images become.

This chapter is not about lighting equipment or technical diagrams. This is about unlocking your creative eye so you know exactly *when* to shoot, *where* to stand, and *how* to use the light you already have.

Natural Light: Your Most Powerful (and Free) Tool

Forget the flash for now. The sun is the most beautiful, dramatic, and forgiving light source you'll ever use—and it's available to you every day.

The trick? Learning how to *read* it.

The Mood of the Day: How Light Changes Over Time

Time of Day Light Quality Ideal golden hour (1 hour after sunrise/before sunset) Soft, warm, directional Portraits, landscapes, mood Midday Harsh, direct, strong shadows Black-and-white, contrast Overcast Soft, even, low contrast Portraits, detail shots **Twilight/Blue Hour** Cool, gentle, moody light Night cityscapes, silhouettes.

> **Pro Insight: The** best light isn't always the brightest. It's the most *thoughtful.*

Direction of Light: How to Shape a Face or a Scene

There are four basic ways light hits your subject:

1. **Front Light** — Light comes from behind you
    - Flattens texture, reduces shadows
    - Easy but often lacks depth
2. **Side Light** — Light comes from the left or right
    - Adds drama, highlights form and texture
    - Best for portraits, architecture, still life
3. **Back Light** — Light comes from behind the subject
    - Creates glow, rim lighting, silhouettes

   - Requires exposure adjustments

4. **Top Light** — Harsh overhead (sun at noon)
   - Strong shadows are not flattering for faces
   - Best avoided for people—move to shade or wait for better timing

> Rule of Thumb: Walk around your subject. Watch how the light changes the emotion. Don't just shoot—*study*.

Soft Light vs. Hard Light

- **Soft light** is diffused, gentle, and wraps around your subject.
  - Found on cloudy days, near windows with curtains, during golden hour.
  - It's flattering, especially for portraits.
- **Hard light** is direct and unfiltered and creates sharp edges and shadows.
  - Found under midday sun, flash, or spotlight.
  - Dramatic, bold, but risky for faces.

Neither is "better"—they tell different stories.
Soft light whispers. **Hard light** shouts.

Indoor Light: Finding Beauty Where You Are

Even at home, beautiful light is all around you—if you know where to look.

Window Light

- Best friend of portrait and still life photographers
- Creates soft side lighting
- Place your subject 45° to the window for dimension

Open Doorways

- Transitional light—bright to dark
- Great for mood and shadow play

Lamps & Overhead Lights

- Often too warm or uneven alone
- Use as creative accents, or bounce with white paper or wall.

> Tip: Turn off **mixed lighting sources** (like daylight + bulb). It confuses white balance and creates color casts.

What About Flash?

Here's the truth: built-in flash is often **too harsh** and **too direct** for natural-looking photography.

- It flattens faces
- Causes red-eye
- Overexposes close subjects, underexposes the background

Do this instead:

- Turn off the flash
- Increase ISO in low light
- Use window or side lamps
- Or bounce a small light off the wall or ceiling

Later, you can explore **external flash**, softboxes, and modifiers. But for now, learning to master **ambient light** is far more powerful.

Light Exercises to Train Your Eye

1. **Follow the Light**
    - Walk around your home at different times of day
    - Notice how the light moves, changes, warms, cools
    - Take photos of the *same object* at morning, noon, and dusk
2. **Shoot in One Window Only**
    - Choose one light source (like a north-facing window)
    - Photograph a person, object, or food

   - Change the subject's angle—see how shadows evolve

3. **Backlight Something**
   - Hold an object (like a leaf or glass) between you and the sun
   - See what happens when light passes *through* it
   - Try silhouettes at sunset with your subject between you and the light

Bonus Tip: How to Find the Best Light Instantly

Here's a secret professionals use all the time:

Hold out your hand and slowly rotate it in the light.

Watch how shadows fall across your fingers.
You'll instantly see where the light is softest, most dramatic, or most flattering. That's where your subject should be.

Final Thought: Light Is Emotion

Think about your favorite photos—the ones that made you feel something.

Chances are, it wasn't just the subject. It was the way the light danced across their face. The warmth of the sky. The way shadows curved around the edges.

That's what light does. It tells the truth of the moment.

> You don't need expensive tools. You just need to *notice*. Because once you can see the light… you can shape it. And once you can shape light, you can shape emotion.

And with light as your language, you're ready to take on the most timeless, meaningful subject of all:

People.

Chapter 6

Portraits & People — Creating Emotion and Connection

Photographing people is about more than lighting and focus. It's about connection. It's about trust. It's about making someone feel *seen.*

When you photograph a person—whether it's a loved one, a stranger, or yourself—you're not just recording an image. You're holding a moment still. A glance. A softness. A story.

This chapter will teach you how to create portraits that move people. Not just with beautiful light and sharp eyes—but with soul.

Portraits Aren't Just Pictures of Faces

Think of the portraits that have stuck with you:
The weathered hands of a grandparent.
The mischievous smile of a child.
The stillness in a quiet gaze.

None of these were "perfect." But they felt *true.*

Great portraits are not about flawless skin or expensive lenses. They're about creating space for someone's personality to come through—and then pressing the shutter at just the right moment.

The Beginner's Mindset: Don't Aim for Perfection. Aim for Presence.

Forget trying to make someone look like a magazine model. You're not here to create *fake beauty.* You're here to show *real presence.*

Start with one question:

> What do I want this photo to feel like?

Because that answer—not your settings—will shape every choice you make.

Positioning the Person: More Than Just "Pose and Smile"

Many people feel awkward in front of a camera. Your job? Make them feel safe.

- Talk to them. Make them laugh. Let them breathe.
- Keep the camera down until the tension fades.
- Photograph the moments between the poses—the smiles *after* the smile, the glance *after* the laugh.

Now let's walk through the basics of setup.

Distance: Get Closer Than Feels Comfortable

Want a more intimate portrait? **Fill the frame.**
Most beginners stand too far away.

- For headshots, aim to fill the frame with the head and shoulders.
- For environmental portraits (person in their space), step back, but keep them the anchor.

> Tip: Avoid cropping at joints (like elbows, knees, or necks). Crop mid-thigh, waist, or shoulders for more flattering results.

Focus: Eyes Are Everything

If the **eyes** aren't sharp, the portrait won't feel alive.

- Use **Single Point Focus Mode**
- Move the focus point directly over the subject's **eye nearest the camera**
- Use **Single Shot Autofocus** (AF-S or One Shot AF)

> Bonus Tip: With children or pets, set your focus in advance and be ready to shoot fast. They rarely hold still for long!

Light: Soft, Directional, Gentle

For portraits, aim for:

- **Window light from the side**—adds dimension without harshness
- **Golden hour outdoors**—warm, glowing skin tones
- **Shade on sunny days**—avoids harsh shadows under the

eyes and nose

Position your subject so that light **gently skims across** their face from one side.
It should wrap, not flatten.

Angles: Small Shifts, Big Difference

How someone is turned can completely change the mood.

- **Face straight on:** Bold, direct, often serious
- **Chin slightly down:** More dramatic, thoughtful
- **Head turned slightly to the side:** Relaxed, softer feel
- **Looking away from camera:** Contemplative, candid, cinematic

> Experiment. Shoot the same person from above, at eye level, and from slightly below. You'll begin to notice what feels most natural for them—and you.

Hands, Posture, and Natural Gestures

Nothing ruins a portrait faster than "What do I do with my hands?" syndrome.

- Give their hands a purpose: touching a face, in pockets, holding an object, lightly crossed
- Keep their posture relaxed. Shoulders down. Neck tall. No tension.

- Use natural prompts: "Tilt your head slightly. Relax your jaw. Think about your favorite place."

> Don't pose. **Prompt.** Instead of saying, "Smile," say, "What would your best friend say if they saw you right now?"

The result is real.

Candid vs. Posed: Let the Person Lead

Some people love being photographed. Others shrink.

- For outgoing people, you can play more with direction, action, and energy.
- For shy or quiet people, give them space. Use long lenses. Step back. Let them forget you're there.

> Candid shots often reveal more truth than any pose. Stay ready between poses. That's where the magic lives.

Group Portraits

Simple guidelines:

- Stagger heights (don't line everyone up like bowling pins)
- Keep everyone at roughly the same **focal plane** so they stay sharp
- Use a **higher f-stop** (like f/5.6 to f/8) to keep all faces in focus

- Focus on **someone near the center**, and **shoot multiple frames**—someone always blinks!

Practice Exercise: The 10-Minute Portrait

Find someone willing to help you practice—friend, partner, or child.

- Choose soft natural light (near a window or outdoors in shade)
- Take 10 photos from different angles and distances.
  - One looking at camera
  - One looking away
  - One smiling naturally
  - One not smiling at all
  - One close-up of just their hands or face detail

Review each photo. Ask yourself:

- Which feels the most like *them*?
- What expression made *you* feel something?

That's your real work. And you just did it.

Final Thought: A Portrait Is a Gift

When someone lets you photograph them, they're giving you something deeply personal.

Your job isn't to perfect them—it's to reflect them.
To show them what's beautiful about them, often without them realizing it.

> Great portraits don't demand attention.
> They whisper something honest.
> And honesty, photography, is what lasts forever

Now that you've connected with the human side of photography, it's time to go wide again—bigger, broader, wilder. We're heading into the world of landscapes, travel, and storytelling at scale.

Chapter 7

Landscapes & Travel — Telling Stories Through Scenes

You've probably been there: standing in front of a magnificent view—mountains rising like giants, a golden sky melting into the horizon—and you raise your camera, full of awe… only to later find your photo feels *flat*, dull, and lifeless.

It's not because the place wasn't beautiful.
It's because capturing a landscape is about more than pointing and shooting.
It's about seeing how *light, timing, composition, and emotion* all work together in harmony.

This chapter will teach you how to translate that moment—*the wind, the stillness, the scale*—into an image that actually moves someone.

Landscapes Are More Than Scenery

Whether you're photographing a forest trail, a city skyline, or a quiet beach—landscape and travel photography are about **presence.**

It's not just *what* you shoot.
It's **when** you shoot. **Where** you stand.

What you choose to include.
And **how** you make someone else feel like they were standing beside you.

The Essentials of a Great Landscape

To consistently take powerful scenic shots, keep these four elements in mind:

1. Light—direction, warmth, softness

2. Composition—What leads the eye? What tells the story?

3. **Foreground Interest—**What anchors the scene?

4. Timing—time of day, time of year, the *decisive moment*

Let's explore each one.

The Light Makes or Breaks the Scene

The best landscapes are lit *beautifully*, not just brightly.

- **Golden Hour (1 hour after sunrise/before sunset):**
  Soft, warm, low-angle light adds depth and texture to everything it touches.

- **Blue Hour (twilight):**
  Cool, ethereal light creates moody, atmospheric photos—great for lakes, mountains, and cities.

- **Midday:**
  Often the hardest time to shoot. Light is flat, harsh, and unforgiving unless clouds soften it.

Tip: Be where you want to shoot **before** the light is perfect. Moments pass fast.

Composition Tricks for Bigger Impact

You already know the **Rule of Thirds**, but landscapes demand more:

Layering (Foreground – Midground – Background)

Think of your image as a stage with three parts:

- **Foreground** gives the viewer a place to enter the scene
- **Midground** shows the story
- **Background** reveals the setting, the sky, the scale

Add rocks, flowers, footprints, and branches in the foreground—even small things matter.

Leading Lines

Use roads, rivers, fences, or paths to guide the viewer's eye into the scene.

Reflections

Still water? Lean into it. Reflections double the interest.
Shoot just after sunrise or before sunset when the water is calmest.

Frame Within a Frame

Use arches, branches, windows, or cliffs to "frame" your scene and add visual depth.

The Power of Human Scale

Want to make a vast landscape feel even more epic?
Place a person in it—*small*, distant, almost like a dot.

- This contrast shows the **grandeur of nature**
- It adds a **sense of story and place**
- It helps viewers imagine themselves in the scene

> A red jacket, umbrella, or silhouette works great for contrast.

Wide Isn't Always Better

Yes, landscapes often call for **wide-angle lenses** (10–24mm on crop sensor, 16–35mm on full frame).

But here's the catch: wide angles can make distant scenes feel even *smaller* if not composed carefully.

- Use wide angles to emphasize *depth*—not just width.
- Get low. Bring in foreground elements. Fill the frame with

meaning.

> Don't just shoot wide—shoot **with intent.**

Travel Photography: Beyond the Postcard

Travel photography isn't just about landmarks. It's about **culture, rhythm, color, light, people, textures, food, and quiet moments.**

Try this:

- Photograph locals *from a respectful distance* (or ask permission)
- Capture signs, doorways, alleyways, laundry lines
- Tell the story of a morning market, not just the church tower

> Travel photos become timeless when they focus on **details,** not just destinations.

Travel & Landscape Shooting Tips (You'll Actually Use)

- **Use a Tripod** at sunrise/sunset or in low light (even a mini one)

- **Shoot in RAW** to capture dynamic range for later editing
- **Use a Polarizing Filter** to deepen skies and reduce glare on water/leaves
- **Set Focus Manually** for distant subjects if autofocus struggles
- **Use a Narrow Aperture (f/8–f/16)** for full sharpness across the frame
- **Bracketing:** Take 3 versions of the same shot at different exposures.

> Always shoot a little wider than needed—you can crop later, but you can't addhat wasn't there.

The Patient Photographer Sees the Best Light

The difference between a good photo and a breathtaking one? **Waiting.**

- Waiting for the clouds to break
- Waiting for the wind to calm
- Waiting for a person to walk into the perfect spot
- Waiting for the sky to turn fire-red for just 10 seconds—and being ready

Don't rush. Let the scene reveal itself. That's how you capture *what it felt like* to be there.

Final Thought: You're Not Just Taking Photos. You're Documenting Wonder.

Every place you go, there's a story waiting to be told—not just of what you saw, but how it felt.

- The silence before the sun rose
- The wind that shook the grass
- The way the light kissed the water and disappeared

And *you*—with a camera in your hand—are the one who brings that story back to the world.

> Don't just document your travels. Let them change the way you see.
> And then, with patience and love, share that seeing with others.

Chapter 8

Everyday Photography — Finding Beauty in the Ordinary

We tend to think of photography as something you do *out there*. On vacation. At events. During golden hour on a mountaintop.

But the truth is, some of the most moving, timeless photographs in the world were taken in kitchens. On sidewalks. In alleyways. In moments of silence that no one else thought to capture.

This chapter is about opening your eyes—*right where you are.*

You don't need new scenery.
You need new **awareness.**

Rewiring the Way You See

We're all trained to overlook the ordinary.
We walk past the same chair, the same doorway, and the same shadows every day—and stop seeing them.

But the camera doesn't care what's familiar.
It doesn't know that a cracked wall or a beam of light on the floor is "nothing special."
It only records what *you choose to show it.*

And when you slow down enough to *see* again, you start to realize beauty never **left. You just stopped noticing.**

The Foundations of Everyday Artistry

Let's simplify. To make great images in your everyday space, you only need three things:

1. Light—the kind that changes as the day moves
2. Presence—the willingness to pause and look
3. Curiosity—to ask, *"What would this look like through my lens?"*

That's it.

Let's explore how to find and use them all.

Lighting the Unremarkable

Most homes have one or two naturally photogenic corners—and you don't need a studio setup to find them.

Watch for:

- Light hitting the floor through blinds or curtains
- Morning light pouring in across a countertop
- Harsh sunlight casting strong shadows against a wall
- Golden hour light skimming over plants, glass, or skin

Choose one spot. Sit with it. Notice how the light moves across the hour.
You'll begin to see moods you never knew were there.

Composing the Mundane Like a Master

Frame With Purpose

Even simple things become extraordinary when framed with intention.

- A half-eaten breakfast on a worn wooden table
- A child's shoes left at the door
- A coffee mug with steam rising in the morning light

Use everything you've learned—leading lines, negative space, shallow depth of field, symmetry.
Let composition give weight to the moment.

Get Close. Then Closer.

Everyday details hide entire worlds.

- The lines in a palm
- The texture of linen in window light
- A single flower petal about to fall

Macro lenses are great—but you don't need one. Use your kit lens. Zoom. Focus closely. Let texture become the subject.

The Home as a Gallery

Your house, apartment, or even single room can be a stage for photographic exploration.

Try these:

- **Still Life**: Arrange a few items with personal meaning. Shoot from above, then from the side. Use natural light only.
- **Window Portraits:** Have someone stand close to a window. Shoot candidly as they read, sip, and stare. Let the light fall naturally.
- **Reflections:** Use mirrors, glass tables, or even puddles. Create layers. Frame the unexpected.

Street & Neighborhood Photography — The Art of Noticing

You don't need to travel far to practice travel photography. Just step outside.

- Photograph alleyways, bicycles, peeling paint, quiet doorways
- Capture routines: commuters, kids walking home, dogs being walked
- Use reflections in windows, puddles, or car mirrors
- Frame street signs, textures, and layered light

Bonus tip: Go out with one goal. *"Today I'm only photographing shadows."* Limiting your focus unlocks unexpected creativity.

Exercises to Train Your Inner Photographer

1. The 10-Foot Radius Challenge

Pick one room. Take **10 photos** without moving more than 10 feet. Use different angles, light, and compositions.

2. The Color Hunt

Choose one color (red, green, or blue). Spend an hour photographing only things of that color. Indoors or out.

3. Object Storytelling

Pick a single object—a shoe, a spoon, a photo, or a glass.
Create a 3-photo narrative around it. Use light, angle, and depth to imply meaning.

Final Thought: If You Can Photograph the Ordinary, You Can Photograph *Anything*

Most photographers are waiting for "better" conditions.
Better light. Better subjects. Better gear. Better locations.

But the truth is, the best photographers create art with *whatever* is in front of them.

The light on a curtain.
The steam from a kettle.
The glance between two people who thought no one was watching.

You have all the tools you need to make that kind of magic—right now.
You just have to *look again.*

And once you've found that power, you're ready to explore the final layer of photographic expression:

Editing. Not to fix what's broken—but to elevate what's already beautiful.

Chapter 9

Intro to Photo Editing — Enhance Without Overdoing It

A common myth about editing is that it's only for fixing bad photos—or that it somehow "fakes" the reality of an image.

But here's the truth: every professional photo you've ever admired—from a National Geographic landscape to a Vogue cover—has been edited.

Not to deceive.

To **clarify**. To **enhance**. To **finish the sentence,** the camera started.

In this chapter, you'll learn a beginner-friendly editing flow that makes your photos cleaner, more compelling, and more *you*—without ever losing their honesty or natural feel.

Why Edit?

Even the best camera is limited. It doesn't feel emotion. It doesn't know what caught your eye. It records light mechanically.

Editing is where you bring that moment **back to life.**

Good editing does three things:

1. **Restores** what the camera couldn't capture (e.g., shadows, highlights)
2. **Guides** the viewer's eye where you want it to go
3. **Shapes** the mood, tone, and color to match your vision

What You Need to Get Started

You don't need expensive software. In fact, you probably already have everything you need.

If You Edit on a Phone:

- **Snapseed** (Incredible control, non-destructive edits)
- **Lightroom Mobile (Free + paid options)—More** advanced, cloud-based
- **VSCO, Adobe Express, Afterlight—great** for quick tweaks

If You Edit on a Computer:

- **Lightroom Classic/Lightroom CC—**Industry standard, intuitive
- **Capture One Express (Free for Sony/Fuji users**-level color control)
- **Darktable/RawTherapee (Free, open** Deep tools,

learning curve)

- **Apple Photos/Windows Photos**—Basic but usable

Start with what you're comfortable with. Master the basics. Grow later.

RAW vs. JPEG—What's the Difference?

- **JPEG** is processed in-camera. Looks finished. Smaller file.
- Raw is unprocessed. More flexible. Requires editing. Larger file.

> Tip: If your camera supports it, **shoot in RAW + JPEG**. Use JPEGs for quick use. Edit RAWs when you want the full range of control.

The Core Editing Flow (Less Than 10 Minutes)

Let's simplify. Here's a basic editing order to follow that works 90% of the time.

1. Crop & Straighten

- Remove distractions
- Adjust horizon lines (especially in landscapes)
- Consider Rule of Thirds, negative space, symmetry

2. Exposure & Contrast

- Brighten or darken as needed
- Add contrast for depth and punch
- Watch for blown-out highlights or crushed shadows

3. Highlights & Shadows

- Pull down highlights to recover sky or skin tones
- Lift shadows to reveal detail in darker areas
- Don't go too far—keep it natural

4. White Balance/Color Temperature

- Cool down overly orange shots
- Warm up photos taken in the shade
- Use warmth to set emotional tone

> Tip: A warmer photo feels intimate. A cooler one feels distant or modern. Use color to match the *feeling*.

5. Clarity, Texture, Sharpness

- Increase clarity for punch (especially in nature and detail shots)
- Boost texture for fabric, skin, surfaces

- Use sharpening subtly (overdoing it causes noise)

6. Color

- Boost vibrance (not saturation) for natural skin tones
- Tweak individual colors to enhance mood (e.g., turn greens richer, blues cooler)
- Desaturate backgrounds to highlight subject

The Before & After Test

Every few edits, **toggle the "before/after" view** (most apps have this).

Ask yourself:

- Is the photo clearer?
- Is the focus stronger?
- Does it feel more like what I *felt* when I took it?

If not—undo, refine, or simplify.

Presets: Helpful, But Not a Shortcut to Vision

Presets (or filters) are pre-made edits you can apply in one click.

They can be great **starting points**—but they're not magic.

- Use a preset → then fine-tune based on *your* image
- Don't apply blindly across all photos

- Build your own signature preset as you develop your style

Remember: **A preset is not your style. Your eye is.**

Practice Project: The One-Image Edit

Choose one image you've taken recently that feels *almost great.*

1. Open it in your preferred editor
2. Follow the flow: crop → exposure → contrast → highlights/shadows → color
3. Save three versions:
    - Slightly edited
    - Fully edited
    - Over-edited (just for fun)

Compare them side-by-side. Which one *feels* like the truth?
You're not just learning how to edit. You're learning how to decide.

Final Thought: Editing Isn't a Fix. It's a finish.

Editing is not where you "rescue" bad photos. It's where you **finish the vision** that started the moment you lifted the camera.

- It's a painter's final strokes.
- A musician's mastering session.

- A writer's edit before publishing.

> When done right, it's invisible.
> When done well, it enhances the emotion, not just the exposure.

And now that you've learned to shoot, compose, light, and edit, it's time to think bigger.

What do you *do* with your photography?
How do you grow? Share? Curate your best work.

That's what we'll explore in the next chapter.

Chapter 10

Building Your Photography Confidence & Style

By now, you've learned the fundamentals—exposure, focus, light, composition, and editing. You've practiced. You've made mistakes. You've captured a few moments that surprised even you.

And now comes the most personal step:
Turning all of that into **your voice**—the kind of photographer only *you* can be.

But to get there, we have to talk about something that every beginner struggles with, yet few books ever address: **self-doubt.**

Why Confidence Is the Real Secret Skill

Ask any professional photographer—no matter how talented—and they'll tell you this:

"There were years when I doubted every photo I took."

Photography is vulnerable. You're putting your perspective out into the world.
It's natural to feel like you're not good enough or that your photos aren't "as great" as others online.

But here's the thing:

- Your journey is *yours.*
- Your eye is *yours.*
- And confidence doesn't come from praise. It comes from *practice.*

How to Build Confidence With Intention

Confidence isn't ego. It's **trust in your ability to improve.** Here's how to strengthen that trust, step by step.

1. Create Consistently (Even When It's Boring)

Don't wait for a perfect scene. Photograph *something* every day. Consistency builds fluency—like learning a new language.

2. Review Your Work Regularly

Every few weeks, revisit your recent photos.

- What patterns do you notice?
- What made you feel proud?
- What do you wish you'd done differently?

This reflection is where growth happens.

3. Keep an "I Got It" Folder

Every time you take a photo that feels special, save it in a dedicated folder.
These are your confidence builders. Return to them when you forget how far you've come.

4. Join a Photography Community

Find an online group, local meetup, or forum.
Not to compare—but to connect, share, and learn.
Feedback is fuel when it comes from the right place.

Curating Your Work Like a Storyteller

Taking a great photo is one skill.
Choosing your best ones? That's another entirely.

Here's how professionals curate:

- **Shoot wide, edit narrow.** Only keep the strongest frames.
- **Create photo sets** that explore a mood, theme, or subject.
- **Think in "triptychs"**—sets of 3 photos that tell a micro-story.
- **Ask: Would I print this? Would I show this in a gallery?**

> Tip: If you're emotionally attached to a photo, ask someone else to review it. They'll see what you're too close to notice.

Finding and Evolving Your Style

Let's demystify this:

Style is not a preset.
It's not a certain lens or editing "look."
It's your instincts, your eye, and your curiosity—revealed over time.

Here's how to recognize it:

- What subjects keep calling you back?
- What kind of light do you love most?
- What feelings do your best photos carry?
- What colors, angles, or moments feel *right* to you?

You don't pick a style. You shoot, you reflect, and one day… you realize it's already there.

How to Keep Growing (Forever)

Photography is not something you finish learning. It's something you live with.

Here are practices that keep the spark alive:

- **Shoot with constraints.** (Only black and white.). Only one lens. Only strangers.)
- **Study the masters.** (Gordon Parks. Vivian Maier. Sebastiao Salgado. Sally Mann.)

- **Print your photos.** Touch them. Frame them. See what they look like off-screen.
- **Teach someone else.** You'll realize how much you know when you share it.

The Photographer's Manifesto (Yours to Keep)

I will slow down.
I will shoot with curiosity, not judgment.
I will make bad photos and keep going.
I will look for light, even in shadow.
I will photograph what I love, not what others expect.
I will return to scenes others walk past.
I will learn to trust my eye.
I will create without apology.
I will remember why I started.

Final Thought: You Are the Photographer You Were Looking For

You don't need permission.
You don't need more followers.
You don't need "better" equipment.

You need only to keep going.
To shoot with honesty. To edit with love.
To look at the world—not as a backdrop, but as a story waiting for your voice.

You are not just taking pictures anymore.
You are building a body of work.
You are becoming a visual author.

And the story you're writing—with every frame—is one the world needs to see.

Chapter 11

BONUS CHAPTER

25 Photography Challenges to Reinforce What You've Learned

At this point, you've learned more than enough to begin making images with depth, power, and purpose.

But here's the truth that separates the readers from the artists:

> Practice isn't what you do after you learn photography.
> It's how you learn photography.

This chapter is your bridge—from knowledge to instinct, from theory to mastery.

Below, you'll find 25 challenges. You can do them in any order, at your own pace. You can repeat them. Modify them. Turn them into personal projects.

Each one is designed to:

- Deepen your creative eye
- Build confidence in your camera handling
- Train your brain to see the invisible magic in everyday life

Let's begin.

The Challenges

1. One Room, 10 Shots

Stay in one room for 20 minutes. Take 10 compelling, unique photos—changing only your angle, distance, or composition.

2. Portrait Without a Face

Photograph a person in a way that tells a story—without showing their face. Hands, posture, clothing, or silhouette.

3. Follow the Light

Pick one spot in your house. Photograph it at five different times during the day as the light changes.

4. The Color Hunt

Choose a single color. Photograph only things in that color for one full day—indoors, outdoors, wherever you go.

5. Reflection Obsession

Spend a day shooting only reflections—in water, glass, mirrors, metal, or unexpected places.

6. Strangers With Stories

Politely ask someone you don't know if you can photograph them. Capture their portrait and one detail that tells who they are.

7. Silhouette Stories

Use backlighting (sunset, windows, lamps) to shoot strong silhouettes. Don't expose for the subject—expose for the light.

8. Negative Space

Create five images that emphasize empty space around the subject. Let the void speak louder than the object.

9. One Lens Only

Pick one focal length (e.g., 35mm or 50mm). Shoot *everything* with it for 3 days straight—portraits, landscapes, street, and still life.

10. The 1-Minute Challenge

Pick a subject. Give yourself exactly 60 seconds to shoot it—no overthinking, no reshoots. Trust your gut.

11. The 3-Photo Story

Tell a story with just 3 images. Beginning, middle, and end. No captions. Use light and sequence to speak.

12. Shoot Like It's Film

Set a limit: 24 photos only today. No previews, no deletions. Review them at the end—like film.

13. Shoot in Black and White Only

Turn on your camera's monochrome preview. Look for texture, shadow, contrast, and light—not color.

14. Hands as Emotion

Photograph hands—at work, at rest, holding, reaching. Let them carry emotion without words.

15. A Place You Know by Heart

Go to a familiar spot (your kitchen, your street corner). Photograph it as if you've never seen it before.

16. Window Light Portraits

Photograph someone near a window. Use only natural light. Experiment with angles and emotional expressions.

17. The Stranger's Back

Photograph strangers or passersby—*from behind*. Tell a story with posture, environment, and distance.

18. A Day in 6 Frames

Capture your entire day using only six photos. Choose carefully. Think storytelling, rhythm, and contrast.

19. Street Without Faces

Document life on the street without showing anyone's face—just gestures, shoes, shadows, objects, and light.

20. Golden Hour Series

Shoot at golden hour for 7 days straight. Explore what soft light does to skin, sky, buildings, and plants.

21. The 12-Hour Set

Take one photo every hour for 12 hours. Capture moments from waking to winding down.

22. Patterns & Repetition

Find and photograph repeating shapes—tiles, fences, bricks, shadows, and people walking in step.

23. Minimalist Masterpiece

Create one photo with *one subject* and *zero distractions*. Clean, bold, and intentional.

24. Before the World Wakes

Wake up early. Shoot for one hour before sunrise. Capture the mood, the quiet, and the slow emergence of light.

25. The "I Am a Photographer" Project

Create five images that, together, say, This *is who I am as a photographer.*
Use anything you've learned. Don't ask what's popular—ask what's *true.*

Final Words: This Is How Mastery Is Made

You now have the tools.
The knowledge.
The insight.
And the spark.

But mastery doesn't come from reading one book.
It comes from showing up with your camera—again and again.
It comes from learning your voice by using it.
It comes from creating not for likes, but for legacy.

You don't need permission to call yourself a photographer.

If you see. If you shoot. If you care, you already are one.

Now go.
Take the photos no one else can take.
The world is waiting to see through your eyes.

Acknowledgements

Creating this book has been a journey as much about photography as it has been about people—those who stood beside me, believed in the vision, and helped bring it into focus.

First, to the readers—whether you're picking up a camera for the first time or rediscovering your creative spark—thank you. Your curiosity, your hunger to learn, and your desire to capture the world around you are the very reasons this guide exists.

To the photographers who came before me—both legendary and unknown—your work inspired me to see light and shadow differently. You reminded me that the camera is not just a tool but a language.

To my early mentors and friends in the field, thank you for the countless late-night conversations, critique sessions, and shared sunrise shoots. Your insight, encouragement, and challenges helped me evolve from a hobbyist to a teacher.

A special thanks to the online photography communities, forums, and students I've taught—your questions, frustrations, and "aha" moments have shaped the clarity and heart of this guide. You reminded me what it feels like to start at square one.

To the editors, collaborators, and publishing team who helped bring this book to life with polish and purpose—your expertise is deeply appreciated.

Finally, to my family and loved ones—thank you for your patience when I disappeared behind the viewfinder or spent hours writing and refining pages. Your quiet support gave me the space to create freely and finish what I started.

This book is for everyone who ever doubted their creative potential. Here's proof that you don't need expensive gear or years of training—just a desire to learn, a willingness to try, and a spark of imagination.

Thank you for allowing me to be part of your photographic journey.

About the Author

Marc T. Billy is a passionate photographer, educator, and visual storyteller with over a decade of hands-on experience capturing the world through the lens. Known for his ability to break down complex photography concepts into simple, actionable steps, Marc has helped thousands of beginners transform their photography from blurry snapshots to frame-worthy masterpieces.

Marc's journey began not in a studio but in everyday life, where he taught himself the art of natural lighting, composition, and camera mastery through trial, error, and relentless curiosity. His work spans portraiture, landscapes, urban scenes, and lifestyle photography, often focused on finding beauty in ordinary moments.

Driven by a desire to make digital photography accessible to everyone, Marc created the *Digital Photography Guide* series to empower new camera owners, hobbyists, and visual creatives to shoot with confidence—without the overwhelm of technical jargon.

When he's not behind the camera or mentoring aspiring photographers, Marc enjoys exploring hidden locations, experimenting with creative photo challenges, and turning everyday light into extraordinary images.

Marc believes that with the right guidance, anyone can master the camera and tell powerful stories through photographs. His mission is simple: to help you unlock your inner photographer—one frame at a time.

Made in the USA
Monee, IL
05 November 2026

67809051R00049